Moral and Character Education Lectures for Pupils of Primary Schools

Educate Your Children through Explanation

AF259080

Dear Reader,

I had 5 years in volunteering with CAPR (Collegiate Association for the Research of Principles) during my university studies, and this work consists mostly in the effort to convey the most fundamental principles for successful life, moral values, to young people.

I will refer to another book which was very popular even 25 years ago and has brought many good changes to the conscious life of growing genius in virtuous life style, and then, to the big cultural advancement in the society. I am talking about the educational course "My World and I" with three books – "Way of Love", "Way to Unity" and The Book of Guidance for Parents and Teachers, who use this course in their practice.

Educate through Explanation – this is one of the topics, which overview 10 main ideas for moral education given from parents to their children and by teachers in the classroom. I found this approach so applicable with my own way to bring a proper understanding of human values to the pupils and students, and later to my children as well. Being in the sphere of education in the length of 23 years, I made a conclusion, that finding a right approach to share the most important knowledge makes a significant impact on the future of the youth and, along with this, happy and satisfying environment.

"The education of others with demonstrating your own positive example is extremely important, however, it has some limitations. Children are surrounded by some wrong examples. Beside the exponential behaviour, they need a clarification of standards and expectations to them in words. They suppose to see that we, parents and teachers, lead a model life in relation to values, but also they intuitionally wish to know why we do so. To transform our example to effective influential motive for spiritual growth of the children, we need to give them a knowledge, which values and principles are serving as a base for it.

Often parents tried to answer on every question asked, and children did not take it into account. In the modern days, parents do not have a tendency to give answers, or correction to some particular situations, and the children incur losses in their personal development, because they experience a shortage of parental attention and grow with lack of the values foundation to rely on and build their own righteous path. There is a golden middle way: parents can share with children about the life views what they believe in, and do not make very strong statements of its. In this more conscious and deliberate position they are able to teach and persuade, to listen and advice. "

I hope, that You will find something new in this book with moral education lectures, what can be rewarding in the process of ethical education for the young people today.

With big respect to Your work,

Educational psychologist, Erena Svirska-Huish

Table of the Book Content

1. Introduction. A definition of the moral values and principles – page 3

2. The Healthy life style – page 8

3. Guidance against smoking cigarettes – page 13

4. Guidance against using alcohol – page 16

5. Purity of love before marriage, chastity and fidelity in marriage – page 19

6. Building of the beautiful and lasting family relationships. The main principles – page 22

7. Lecture of the gadget dependency and on the value of reading – page 27

A Course of Lectures on the Moral and Character Education for Pupils in Primary Schools:
Guidance for Teachers

The book is addressed to teachers of primary schools who lead lessons on ethics and can use these materials as a guideline for the first step in education of young people in the most valuable principles for life: a sense of responsibility, effort to make a conscious choice toward goodness and healthy life style habits.

The course with 7 lectures explains to young people how to find true original self and develop a character of a loving person who respect others, put practice of original human values as a priority in life and through these important competencies be prepared to create a successful and happy family!

Moral and Character Education Lectures for Pupils of Primary Schools

Lecture 1

Introduction. A definition of the moral values and principles

We live in the world infused with contradictions. When we meet some difficulties, or some misfortune is following us, we tend to think that the quickest way to escape failures is to give-in to the circumstances or to a strongest opinion of the closest surrounding, even if it does not reflect our personal standpoint or resound with our own understanding of the world. This is not a basic rule of the today's world and many people live in harmony nowadays. But we need to learn how to develop our own line of evaluation, what is right and what is wrong, to become a very well developed person.

But if to think about an ideal of a human life, what it's purpose can we put first and how can we measure it?

-   Every person wants to be happy!

Purpose in Life:

Moral and Character Education Lectures for Pupils of Primary Schools

Do we find happiness only when we are pleasing someone else or only when we indulging our temporary desires? How can we choose a right guidance in the life to be a complete and a satisfied person?

To feel our own value and do not crumble from unpleasant surprises, we need to have moral values and principles as the main guiding line to be able to gain good trust from other people and to be recognised as righteous people in the society ourselves.

What are these moral values and principles consist of? It includes character integrity and continuity of the right deeds. It is when we follow some particular table of spiritual laws which are introduced by numerous religions, schools of ethic and philosophies, but are common in the main views. Also it is learning about ourselves and pursuing the path in accordance to the voice of conscience, which is a main compass of our mind and soul, and as a destination we lead our thoughts and actions to goodness.

What kind of person do you want to become? Successful and achieving set goals in life or spoiled and chasing external pleasures? Of cause, we want to become wholesome, kind, prosperous and happy people! That is why we search to become boys and girls, and later young men and women who practice moral values and principles in life.

To Be Successful in Life
we need to know and follow

What are the spiritual laws I was talking about earlier? Spiritual laws are very similar to physical laws. When we search to discover our internal, God's given values which help us to create useful habits, motivate us to the right actions and as a result we gain good and mature character and personality.

Moral and Character Education Lectures for Pupils of Primary Schools

There is a famous saying which underlines such steps:

"Watch your thoughts; its lead to attitudes.

Watch your attitudes; its lead to words.

Watch your words; its lead to actions.

Watch your actions; its lead to habits.

Watch your habits; its form your character.

Watch your character; it determines your destiny."

We decide our life!

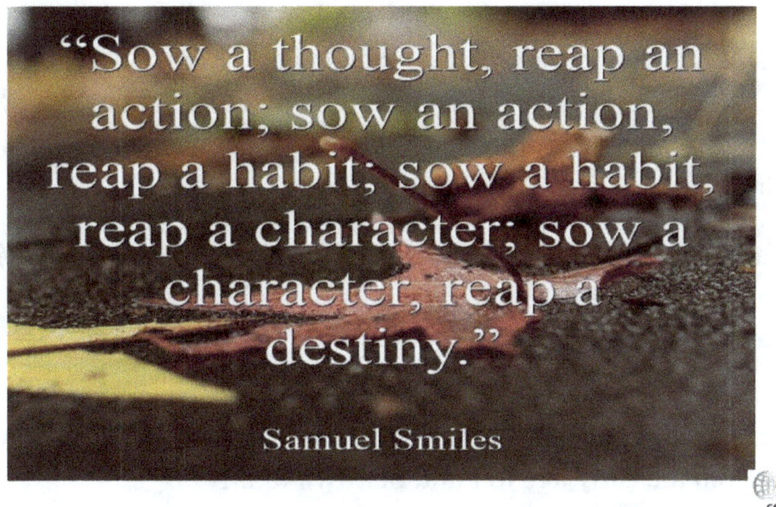

What kind of values do you know?

Which values do you put as a priority?

What kind of goals do you want to achieve?

-    To be a person of True Love!

These are decisive questions to ask ourselves in order to create a view of what kind of life we are going to live. That is why let us think about these questions in this course of lectures which I want to offer to you.

Moral and Character Education Lectures for Pupils of Primary Schools

What we are going to talk about?

1. We will look at the basic principles of healthy lifestyle. Human being is a unique creation who is formed of the mind and body. When we keep our mind and body in the good working order, in unity and harmony, we can live a long and fruitful life. This is the main reason why we need to study what is the healthy life style for our mind and body and to develop right habits helping us in this way.

2. We will talk about a danger of bad habits, such as smoking cigarettes and drinking alcohol. These habits destroy not only our body, but also bring some damage to our ability to think and act constructively. That is why we need to understand which exactly wrong influence bad habits can cause and avoid these habits without any excuse.

3. We will talk about an importance of pure and chaste life style as a source of energy for the internal development and the course to create true joyous relationships with the peers, use it as an opportunity to become a pride for the elders and an excellent example to follow for the younger children.

Your pure relationships of love will become a base for success in creation of future family and raising good children.

4. Next topic of our discussion will be what is a happy family and why we need to prepare ourselves from the early age to build our own family.

When we have a good model of family to imitate and to inherit, we can easily attain the goal of happy and strong family relationships in the future. Knowledge of the main principles and elements of prosperous family and harmonious relationship standard will also guide us to find a proper direction in this sphere of life and to practice the best values.

5. Then we will look at the question of a dependency on the use of high-technological equipment, or gadgets, which make our life easier in many ways, but we need to learn how to dominate over time and use these gadgets smartly in order to prevent spending too much time with its. Instead, we can learn a habit to get necessary information from printed books.

What we would learn:

As a result of this course of lectures I hope and expect, that you can form an understanding for yourselves about what is a really successful life and about the best path to achieve it in your life.

We will follow the way of discovery of a new habit to analyse the advantage of righteousness in life, and we will think about how to develop good practice to be a great person!

Moral and Character Education Lectures for Pupils of Primary Schools

Lecture 2

The Healthy life style

What the healthy life style means and what it consists of?

The answer on this question we can find, if we will look at the main measure of productivity of such a life style - longevity of life.

In present time there are 7.5 billion people in the world, but only a small number of the population of our planet live more than 100 years. Do you know such people?

According to the longevity research, made by the institutions such as the Gerontology Research Group (GRG) or *Guinness World Records*(GWR), the longest human lifespan is that of Jeanne Calment of France (1875–1997), who lived to the age of 122 years, 164 days. As women live longer than men on average, combined records for both sexes are predominated by women.

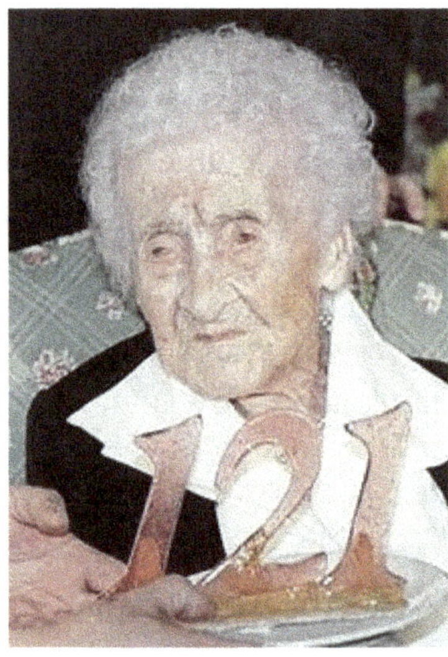

The longest undisputed lifespan for a man is that of Jiroemon Kimura of Japan (1897–2013), who died at age 116 years, 54 days.

Since the death of 117-year-old Chiyo Miyako of Japan on 22 July 2018, 115-year-old Kane Tanaka, also of Japan, born 2 January 1903, is the oldest living person in the world whose age has been documented.

Since the death of 113-year-old Francisco Núñez Olivera of Spain on 29 January 2018, 113-year-old Masazō Nonaka of Japan, born 25 July 1905, is the oldest verified living man in the world.

What is the secret of their long life? You can give your answers!

At whole, if to overview everything what was said before this, we can underline several main moments:

- Healthy eating;
- Positive thinking and attitude in life;
- Denying bad habits;
- Physical exercises and sport;
- Good communication and close connection to relatives and friends.

How much and what do you know about it? Let us think together!

Moral and Character Education Lectures for Pupils of Primary Schools

Healthy eating can include 5 fruit and vegetables a day, drinking water; eating protein and fibre rich foods as well is good but in a healthy variety, and the foods which are usually cooked at home will be very beneficial for your health. If you want to learn how to cook healthy dishes for youself , you can ask your relatives to teach you and participate in the very important everyday rituals of cooking and in this way to help your family and prepare for the future.

Healthy eating means saying 'no' to: a fried, a smoked, a processed food, which are only can be taken as a treat occasionally.

It means to use less of: sugar, sweets, bread and to replace it with natural sources such as honey, fruit, rice cakes as its are easier to digest and have more nutritional value.

It is better to do not use at all the products which contain many chemical-based ingredients and artificial conserving agents.

Positive thoughts and attitude to life.

It is important to keep activity during the day, to have a planned schedule and regular routine of the day and to do not have big disruptions to it. Because these organisational skills bring balance to our emotional state and feelings.

In some sad time or when you experience a failure, take a moment to rest and to analyse the situation and find the positive side of events even in the unpleasant situation. In this way you can create a good plan for your actions, how to continue your activity in order to achieve a victory.

Moral and Character Education Lectures for Pupils of Primary Schools

It is good to have someone very close to you to share your experiences and feelings, to find understanding and support you require.

You can write a diary and register your hopes, feelings, emotions, experiences and later to think about its, make rational conclusions, what can be helpful for you to grow as a person and to develop your success.

Denying of bad habits

You know for sure that smoking cigarettes can cause a cancer of the lungs and using alcohol can create a liver cirrhosis. Bad health brings you to the point when you will have only troubles, worries, financial expenses and limited abilities in your life.

In the relationships of love we also have to make a right choice and keep purity and chastity before marriage for the purpose to avoid a painful result of broken relationship. Because the relationships of love have a very sensitive nature.

As the main principle which we can practice here – we do not need to try those endeavours what can negatively influence on our spiritual or physical existence.

Physical exercises and sport

Beautiful shape of the body attracts a good attention of others, and people who make an effort and train their body win the point, that they experience an emotional lift, they are more productive, easier to concentrate in their everyday work and generally they are more popular among peers.

Moral and Character Education Lectures for Pupils of Primary Schools

Even 5-10 minutes of exercises every morning will bring the substantial changes. More long and constant sport sessions 2-3 times a week will raise our life spirit and improve a resistance to different diseases. It will give us a stimulus to do not give up in front of life challenges. This process of workouts often gives us a sense of comfort and satisfaction. That is why it is important to include an aspect of physical exercises in our schedule of the day and week.

Communication and close connection to relatives and friends

A social survey proved that the relationships with other people have a very big influence on the quality of our life. We can even say, that it is the first and essential need of the person in the row of importance - to be with other people, to feel and experience acceptance and care, to share own thoughts and interests.

Who can help us to make significant in value decisions, to go through a challenging experience, to laugh over a joke, to feel joy of mutual understanding? All of this help can do only the people with whom we have warm and close relationships.

That is why for every person the own family is so crucial part of life, so decisive for our comfort and personal growth. Also we want to keep relationships of friendship with other people.

In this meaning, the best communication we will have with those people for whom we invest and give love unconditionally. This is called the principle of living for the sake of others! Unconditional investment of the heart for other people will give a big satisfaction in the relationships in return. In your future this principle can be leading to achieve success in different spheres of communication, in professional activity, developing a career, establishing own business.

Today we discussed with you general moments of the healthy life style. What was the most important point you remember and ready to take to your life and practice?

-    To develop good habits and create close relationship of heart with people!

This is a very nice understanding! As a part of healthy habits we need to learn to avoid unhealthy habits.

Our next lecture will be about a danger of smoking cigarettes.

Moral and Character Education Lectures for Pupils of Primary Schools

Lecture 3

Guidance against smoking cigarettes

We want to become outstanding and great people and to reach significant results in our life. That is why it is important to determine for ourselves, what is a good way to achieve this goal.

Beforehand, we need to look at the person as a being who exists in two important dimensions: with mind and body. In order to support mind and body cooperation in harmonious unity, we need to care about its well-being.

What is the best nurture or food for our mind? These are reading books, an organised day schedule, positive thought activity, good, caring and kind actions, joyful events and uplifting communication.

What are the necessary conditions for the healthy body? These are right and balanced diet, physical exercises and good external habits.

Moral and Character Education Lectures for Pupils of Primary Schools

To the good habits we put a staying away from bad habits. And smoking cigarettes, drinking alcohol we distinguish as bad habits. If to talk about smoking cigarettes, we need to take attention that it gives a dependency, or addiction. In order to do not fight with the result of this addiction, it is better to do not form this pernicious habit.

We need to understand that smoking cigarettes does not have positive sides, it brings only wasting of money, spoils teeth or make it yellow, clogs the lungs with residue of smoking ash, allows a possibility of lung cancer development. Smoking cigarettes also undermines our social image, as well as brings damage to our physical health.

What do you think about that disapproving and repulsive prints on a cigarette pack, which you can see sometimes on the pavement. To look at those pictures does not bring a good response from our consciousness. But we can understand that such terrible and scary results can be gained after a long use of smoking cigarettes. And we can get an impression that if to use smoking for a short period of time, there would be nothing wrong. In reality this approach is not completely correct.

Even several inhales can influence on our ability to think, to cloud it. After that we cannot analyse and estimate reality well enough, to make thorough decisions. That is why it is better to avoid smoking cigarettes.

What do you know about passive smoking? If you stand next to the person with a burning cigarette, we do not smoke ourselves but we inhale, being drawn in the cigarette smoke or haze. And this fact brings the same effect to our consciousness and blocks our lungs with the smoke micro particles. That is why it is better to ask the person, who is smoking cigarette, to stop this action during your conversation, or to finish communication with him and step aside.

Moral and Character Education Lectures for Pupils of Primary Schools

In this way, if we avoid smoking cigarettes, we can keep our strength, clear thoughts and longevity of our life. If somebody smokes cigarettes in your family, it is better to bring this matter to discussion with the family members and to reach an agreement, that smoking cigarettes person can go outside for that moment, or he or she will stop this habit completely.

From the year 2011 in the United Kingdom, a smoking of cigarettes is officially restricted in public places, such as educational establishments, children's playgrounds, working offices, cafes and restaurants. That is why it is so important to keep this rule in your own house for the sake of well-being and better health of all the family.

So many people dream to change the world. But how can we do it? We can start it by showing a personal example and through this approach to influence on our surrounding.

Non-smoking cigarettes person looks more presentable and prestigious and has much more chances to be popular and to gain a public recognition.

Let us make the right choice and refuse smoking cigarettes for the life time!

Moral and Character Education Lectures for Pupils of Primary Schools

Lecture 4

Guidance against using alcohol

When we meet difficulties in our life, we cannot realise immediately how to overcome its and at times we need to put a lot of effort in place to make an improvement and wait for a certain period for the purpose to achieve a desired results.

That is why, in order not to give in to the circumstances and to effectively deal with life difficulties, we need to work on our character, follow right values and develop good habits, which let us to become successful people.

What is happening when we cannot be strong enough inside our personality and start to flow with the circumstances?

We are experiencing stress and if this state of being does not have it's resolution for a long time, there is a chance that we can become anxious, irritated, embittered.

What is the solution for such a situation?

To find a person who you can share your problem with, who can listen to you, give a good analysis or feedback, or at least will help you to see a current situation from the more positive side of it.

Moral and Character Education Lectures for Pupils of Primary Schools

On the foundation of such an opportunity and having the necessary emotional support, you can gather your internal strength, properly think about the required steps to get an expected outcome and later to fulfil your plan with the best results.

But what can happen if the person does not search for a possibility of support to his or her needs and would not follow such a constructive way? He can be caught by depression, or can come to another danger and start to use alcohol.

At times, we cannot see from the first view, what is happening in the mind of a person, what kind of emotions he or she experience. That is why it is so important to be attentive to our own feelings to be able to recognise the feelings of the people around us, to be kind, to support good deeds and initiatives, to bring positive influence, to do yourself and encourage other people for the heartfelt communication in order for everyone to be happy.

Some people can be lonely and lose true sense of their surrounding, if they do not have such support or uplifting connection with other people. Some people can meet big difficulties in their lives, be suppressed by misunderstanding.

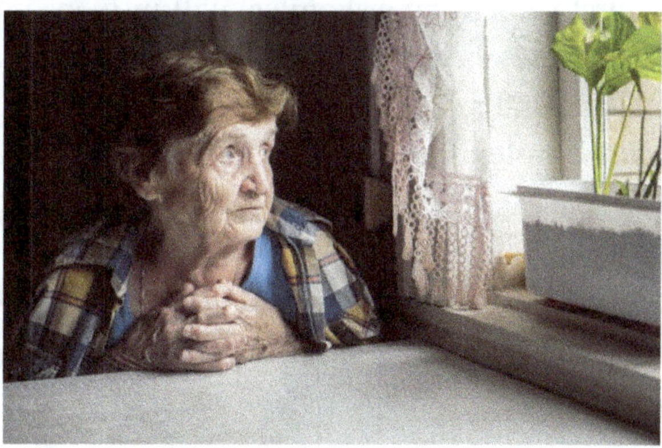

When the people try to get away from such painful reality and make mistake by starting a bad habit – drinking alcohol, this habit can grow to an addiction. People, who tried alcohol once, can feel certain relief, but it cannot give a right solution to existing life problems. What can happen instead with a long term use of alcohol - it can bring disturbance to a physical health – stomach upset, raised blood pressure, and even longer use can cause a liver failure. On the other side of bad effects from alcohol use is a chronic depression.

What is most important, we need to understand that alcohol even in small doses can give an illusion that difficulties will go away by itself, that we would not have negative consequences, somehow we can get an impression, that everything is fine.

Nevertheless, we must reject such an idea and get the proper comprehension how to solve the life difficulties effectively and bring joyful events in life, and positively influence on our surrounding, and achieve the best results in the family, in a career, in self-development and perfection.

Moral and Character Education Lectures for Pupils of Primary Schools

And if you want to learn how to deal with life difficulties effectively, you need to find a trusted elder person – your father if you are a boy, or your mother if you are a girl, in analogy your elder brother or sister, your teacher. This person should be able to listen to you, to give a good advice or share an experience, to show a great life example.

Often when people grow up, most significantly the role model with high life achievements, following moral values and principles, will influence through their whole life and will help to succeed with these good and important values. If we are grown out from one role model, we still can treasure and respect that person but at the same time to direct our life standards, aligning with another role model with higher spiritual level and life principles.

In this way we will develop ourselves constantly and will not experience stagnation. This tactic will help us to overcome unstable situations and have the opportunity to do not give up in difficult situations.

Let us determine for ourselves goals in life – the ones which are pursuing goodness, and choose constructive methods for its fulfilment.

Moral and Character Education Lectures for Pupils of Primary Schools

Lecture 5

Purity of love before marriage, chastity and fidelity in marriage

Life of the person holds a great value, we need to find this attitude in our early years and treasure it during the life time. Even if we did not have a very exciting experience with it previously and meet many adverse situations, we can make an effort to see ourselves from a positive side and realise our God's given value. We can try to find a descriptive image of a true person and with the purpose to reach such standard ourselves, make an effort to understand it in details.

What is the ideal of a person? We want to reach individual perfection, become a developed and successful person, to build a happy and harmonious family and to achieve an external prosperity through the development of business or creating career and gaining recognition in a society.

We already talked about character development and formation of the good habits, what becomes the way of self-perfection. Now we can talk about how to create a happy family, which can exist during your life time since the date of marriage, and you will live with your spouse – husband or wife – in unity and beautiful understanding even in eternity!

Moral and Character Education Lectures for Pupils of Primary Schools

The most important quality in the family is a loyalty to each other. How to develop such quality of the character and prepare yourself for the lifetime commitment to your spouse? We need to discover for ourselves the definition of purity of love before marriage.

What does it mean to live with the intention to be loyal to only one person in love – your future wife or husband? On the foundation of development of such a determination and commitment to such an ideal of relationship, we will definitely achieve the goal of unity, shared love and mutual understanding between spouses.

In other words, purity of love can be called a chastity. This word includes two meanings – wholeness and wisdom, fulfilment and keeping your internal dignity.

A person, young man or woman, who practice such a life style, will gain a respect from the side of their peers and classmates, and by building a positive foundation, will aim a mature character and guaranteed happiness in the future.

That is why it is so important to lead a chaste life style and keep purity, to build relationships with peers as with brothers and sisters.

When the time will come and you will be ready to create your own family, on the base of this important habit you will be able to endlessly respect each other with your spouse and you will live many happy years together!

Your children, by seeing your blissful example, will be inspired to keep their purity of love before marriage and in their turn will also build happy and strong families.

The Value of Marriage = Happiness

And then our society will be filled with very nice families, and as it is well-known, family is a central building stone and the source of good strive, prosperity and flourishing in the society.

Arnold J. Toynbee, a historian who searched for the pattern in the development of different civilizations, made a very important discovery: that the culture of a nation gets to its most welfare and power when an institution of family relationships takes the most profound significance in it. If the family relationships are built on the trust and devotion of husband and wife to each other, loyalty and filial piety of parents and children, this family will be happiest and most successful of all! By inheriting and adapting this model within the society, loyalty and service of government and people within a particular nation will bring a high development to this nation. We can see that the family unit is a small model of the society.

Let us understand the value of a family and importance of devoted relationships within the family. And we can start to prepare ourselves to the building of a consistent relationships and happy marriage by creating the right relations with our peers as with brothers and sisters; with elders around us as with our parents, keeping respect; with younger people around us as with our younger brothers and sisters, practicing care.

In this way our life will change for the better and we can find ourselves as a part of one big family of humanity in our present time and will build together our wonderful future!

Moral and Character Education Lectures for Pupils of Primary Schools

Lecture 6

Building of the beautiful and lasting family relationships

The main principles

In the previous lectures we looked into the vision how important it is to have a preparation to create a family, to nurture the right attitude, self value as the children of God and respect to other people through the development of good personal habits and positive skills in communication with other people.

Also we talked about a preciousness of the family relationships for the own life and life in the society.

What kind of principles will help us to practically implement a harmony, mutual understanding and happiness in the family? We can list several such principles and then I will explain it in some important details.

1. Purity of love before marriage

Purity of Love

2. Fidelity in marriage

3. Love and respect

4. Establishing of good family traditions: for example, to eat meal with a whole family at least one time during the day

Good Family Traditions

5. Pleasant time spending with all family members, joy, humour and laugh

Family Time

6. Unique one-to-one time with parents for the each child, and especially for spouses to deepen a bond with each other and uplift each other's value.

7. Forming and discussion of family plans together and building the activity in mutual support

Moral and Character Education Lectures for Pupils of Primary Schools

If we would approach the development of human history, we will see that a family unit serves as a source of moral and ethical standards; within a family is the basis of religious faith, the ways of learning about this world, traditions and customs are passed from generation to generation, the family unit holds everything what is most important in the life of a person. Precisely in a family people comprehend the value of personal integrity, loyalty, faithfulness and unselfish love.

A person can experience all types of love in a family: love of children, brothers and sisters' love, spousal love and parental love. For the purpose to accomplish this purpose, the family shall include three generations, that all the types of love could exist together and be inherited by the next generation.

In a good family the elders are in the most significant and respectful position. Middle and young members of the family seek advice from them, especially in concern of family traditions and habits. In this sense the elder generation are the keepers of treasure box of kind rituals and useful family habits. They have responsibility for the prosperity of their descendants. For the children it is easier to talk to their grandfather or grandmother than to father or mother, and parents also run to their help when some difficulties arise.

In the centre of a family is a middle generation, or parents; they are governors of the present time and decide a direction of the family life. Their life style is very important for the education of their children and growth of love between husband and wife. If they argue with each other, the family relationships can be spoilt and the future generation will experience difficulties later as well.

Children are the hope for a brighter future, as for their parents, as for the elders in the family. All parents want their children to be better than them, they think about children as their future inheritors, who will fulfil their dreams. However, as much parents want to educate their children in the best possible way and give them good opportunities, they cannot live the life instead of their children.

We came to a conclusion that a family is a unity of three generations. Nobody alone can fully realise the true potential as a person and reach spiritual perfection. We need to be guided by the main principle of life – to live for the sake of others, only then, in good interaction with other people, the harmony, spiritual advancement, joy and happiness can come to us as a result! When we live for others, investing in our family, friends and society all our heart, we will not only give help to those people, but also develop our good life standards and big ability to love.

Moral and Character Education Lectures for Pupils of Primary Schools

Lecture 7

Lecture of the gadget dependency and on the value of reading

We have to strive and develop our ability to think and analyse, train ourselves in creating good and balanced decisions.

If to talk about gadgets, an electronic equipment, it has a purpose to help us and to assist in our study and work process. But using its we shall not come to the point of dependency, to let ourselves be overridden by the time spent with its.

We live to become an owner of our life that is why we need to put constant effort to reach prosperity and success. Because nowadays Internet and social web pages hold so big volume of information, if we are not selective and rational, we can have a difficulty to manage all this massive of words and images. Spending too much time with electronic games can influence on the way how quick we think and react, this habit also can take a form of dependency from getting information in electronic view.

On the opposite, the reading of printed books can allow us to build logical chains of constructive thoughts, beautiful and wholesome vision of the world and enrich our knowledge significantly. Then, our communication with people will grow to much more insightful and pleasant level, our erudition will become better, we will gain more confidence, widen horizon of harmonious perception and develop our creative abilities.

Moral and Character Education Lectures for Pupils of Primary Schools

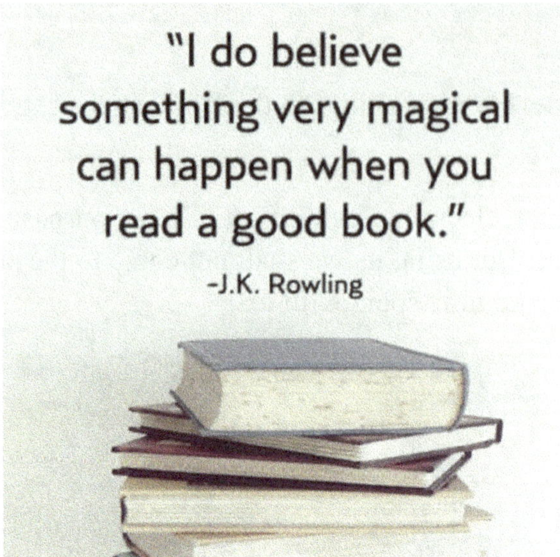

In this way, the more practice and mental exercise we give to our consciousness and thoughts, the more merit we receive, because this is how we can develop speed and effectiveness of our intellectual gifts. We will be a very pompous and interesting companion in conversation, and most importantly, that constant practice and training of the thinking process will bring to a longer use of our intellect on a high level during life time, will open broadly our possibilities such as getting good job, writing books and even for scientific discoveries.

We will still use mobile phones and computers, other electronic devices, mostly not for entertainment but wisely for the purpose of learning and realising our big life dreams.

When we will clearly establish what we want to achieve, what will inspire us and will lead us to the most significant goal in life, then we will concentrate our time and effort easier for the purpose to reach it. That is why we need to search and analyse properly, what kind of life aspiration will be most important for the purpose to make good decisions for your future.

And in the present time we need to study, to read many good books on various subjects, to try a number of different rewarding activities, hobbies and occupations for the purpose to learn and make a right choice for the potential profession, or sphere of development in your main planned activity in life.

Moral and Character Education Lectures for Pupils of Primary Schools

The sources used to accompany the main lecture material:

Wikipedia – about longest living people on Earth.

Google search – for most of the illustrations:

Graduation photography/Zoomix Studio – page 15;

Belle, from Beauty and the Beast movie -https://www.boredpanda.com/belle-gold-dress-emma-watson-beauty-and-the-beast – page 19;

A happy family photo – 123RF.com – page 20.

Space for Your Notes or Reflection

Plan of Lessons Set Up

Results Achieved Due Lecture Work with Pupils

MORAL AND CHARACTER EDUCATION LECTURES FOR PRIMARY SCHOOLS: GUIDANCE FOR TEACHERS

The book is addressed to the teachers of primary schools who lead lessons on ethics and can use these materials as a guideline for the first step in education of young people in the most valuable principles for life: a sense of responsibility, effort to make a conscious choice toward goodness and healthy life style habits.

The course with 7 lectures explains to young people how to find true original self and develop a character of a loving person who respect others, put practice of original human values as a priority in life and through these important competencies be prepared to create a successful and happy family!

ISBN 978-164606966-8